D1333155

THE GLADNESS OF BIRDS

Poems by Irene Howat

Photos by Pat Lomax

With best wishes,

Irene Howat

British Library Cataloguing in Publication Data:

a catalogue record for this publication is available from the British Library

ISBN   978-1-912052-61-5

Typeset in 12.5 Book Antiqua at Haddington, Scotland

Printed by the Book Factory

Photos on page 7 are © Andrew Heaney and John Davidson, and on page 35 © Ron Macdonald, with thanks to all of them

Contents

On the Shoreline

Turnstones fidget the shoreline
pebbling their way,
incongruous in orange stockings
and business beaks,

leaving a trail
of upturned stones
and pinging echoes.

An oystercatcher looks on
elegant,
disapproving.

They Were There

In the clear light of an Orkney afternoon
we set out to find arctic tern,
the greatest migrants in the world.

Then from nowhere
the mist came in,
fold after fold wrapped the cliffs at Birsay.
All we could see were flashes of movement
slicing the mist.

But we heard them,
they were there,
there all around us.

Goldcrests

We did nothing to deserve the visit.
They just came,
a little flight of tiny birds
with pompom bodies
and coal chip eyes.

Crowned with gold crests
– royal visitors indeed –
they graced our garden
for just a few minutes
of beauty in miniature.

Soaring and Wheeling

They laugh at me
the gulls
as I struggle
earthfast
against the wind.

Chortling and cackling
soaring and wheeling
they abandon themselves
to the wind
never dreaming
their feet
will ever touch the ground
again.

The Gannet

From the shore I watched a gannet
wheeling in slow circles,
scanning the sea.

I saw him focus on a pinpoint,
tighten his circle
and change
from graceful bird to lethal weapon.

Not a splash was there
when he sliced through the water
and the fish knew nothing
again.

The Pied Wagtail

In your black suit,
white shirt and smart black shoes
you look every bit the business man.

Black hair slicked back
and black eyes alert
there is no compromise with you.

Obviously in charge, you march
from here to there,
stopping mid-way to check
some urgent item on your list.

Up and down, never at peace.
Places to go, things to do,
the Chief Executive
of the public park.

Comic of the Northern Seas

Comic of the northern seas
the puffin waddles awkwardly
on his bright orange legs.

Wings whirling
like a clockwork toy,
the comic of the northern seas
flies to his cliff-top burrow.

But in the water
he is the supreme swimmer,
the powerful pursuer,
the fiendish fisher.

Sand-eels don't stand a chance
for the comic of the northern seas
has a puffling to feed
and that's no joke.

A Work of Art

The owl
is a study in raw sienna,
burnt umber and cadmium yellow.
No line defines
his edges.

The owl
is woven from autumnal adjectives.
On adverbial wings he glides
slowly, silently, stealthily,
attacking his prey
with exclamation marks.

The owl
is a melody in E flat
that waits estinto,
flies a capella
and swoops precipitato.

There is no repeat.

The Heron

standing still
stock still
steely
staring
statue

fin flip
fatal slip
flash
splash

fish dish

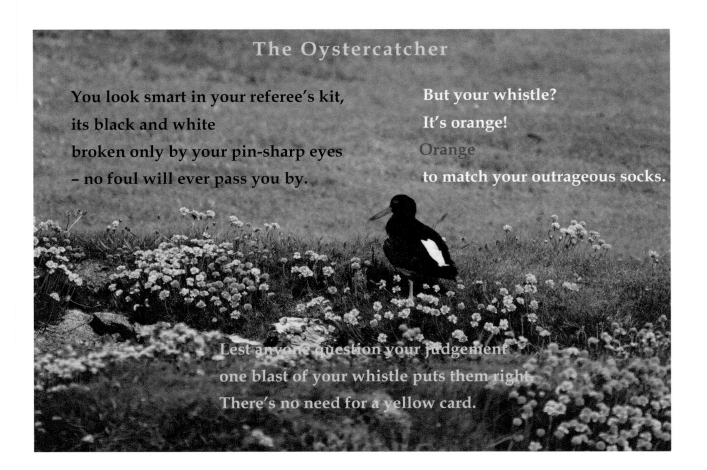

The Oystercatcher

You look smart in your referee's kit,
its black and white
broken only by your pin-sharp eyes
– no foul will ever pass you by.

But your whistle?
It's orange!
Orange
to match your outrageous socks.

Lest anyone question your judgement
one blast of your whistle puts them right.
There's no need for a yellow card.

To a Kingfisher

Do you know that kingfisher blue does not exist,
that your feather jacket
is not what you see reflected in the river?

When you look at your dazzling mate
do you know that she,
like you,
is wearing the emperor's new clothes?

Beautiful you are, but not with your own beauty.
You are what you reflect:
blazing sunlight and radiant sky.
You are rushing waters;
you are the silver fish
you hold in your bill.

Do you know that when you preen yourself,
tucking each blue feather underneath its
         neighbour,
you are living a lie,
you are not what you seem to be?

(The kingfisher has no blue pigment in his feathers.
His blue is reflected light.)

Goldfinch

What will I call you, which of your names?
Goldfinch, red cap, thistle finch,
King Harry?
Right royal you are
with your Midas stripes,
and your ermine waistcoat
in winter.

No ordinary food for you,
royal guest.
Your pin-sharp beak
is made for finer things –
plucking thistle crowns,

pricking teasles,
prising seeds
from feeders made to puzzle
common garden birds.

There is nothing common about you,
King Harry.

To a Treecreeper

You are the mouse of the bird world
as you jerk and shuffle your spiralling way
up and round each tree.

Mousey in your movements,
mousey in your colour
and mousey in your timid ways,
you spiral on.

Pressing your tail against the tree
for balance
you use your long sharp bill
to winkle out insects, all unsuspecting.

And when you reach the top
you fly down to ground level
and begin your life's spiral
all over again.

Curlews

Keepers of moors and memories
your call
is weeping set to music.

Are you remembering
the fires that burned our cottages,
the sheep that filled our land
instead of people?

If our children's children come
looking for an idyll,
call to them.

Call out to them.
Tell them the truth.

To My Blue Tit

You are small, like most gymnasts,
and you wear the smartest
of leotards,
blue and green on the back,
yellow in front,
and all topped off
with a jaunty blue cap.

One moment you are upright,
the next you cartwheel
in a swirl on colour.
I watch as you
twist and turn
and loop the loop
and swing and swoop
on your peanut trapeze.

Magpies

One for sorrow
You have a bad reputation
in fantasy and fact
for filching sparkling treasures
and raiding songbirds' nests
of eggs . . .
and worse.

Two for joy
Handsome and impeccable
masterminds of the bird world
you stride jauntily along roof ridges,
flutter and then glide effortlessly,
showing off your bold pied plumage
to your plain black corvid cousins.

Ten for a bird you must not miss
Late winter finds you in parliament
where your loud laughing chatter
keeps the opposition in its place.
You rule the roost.

Swallows

The swallows flew south
taking summer's blue light
with them
all the way back to Africa.

Bracken-covered hillsides,
bushes and trees
blazed with colours
Moses still remembers,
and they were not consumed.

A leaf fell,
a solitary leaf
fluttered to the ground.

Others followed
in peaceful ones and twos
and stormy thousands
until the tree stood
stark and naked
in the teeth of winter's gales,
yet it was not consumed.

And the swallows
will fly north
once again.

To a Blackbird

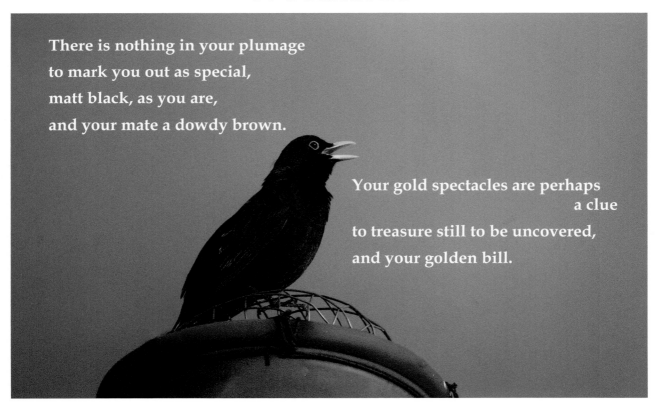

There is nothing in your plumage
to mark you out as special,
matt black, as you are,
and your mate a dowdy brown.

Your gold spectacles are perhaps
a clue
to treasure still to be uncovered,
and your golden bill.

Come spring your treasures flow
in golden arias
and songs of golden waters flowing,
of golden raindrops falling.

        Surprised at yourself you trill
        with laughter that melts
        into golden silence
        in the still spring air.

                Through your spectacles
                she doesn't look dowdy at all.

Wren

You were there today as usual,
appearing out from behind a bush
to find your breakfast
of insects too small for me to notice.

You don't go far, little wren,
along the back border
a matter of yards,
but you come from travelling stock.

Clever people have worked out
that several million years ago
your ancestors came from America
travelling by a roundabout route.

North they went,
going just a matter of yards
and often staying for generations
without moving on at all.

From Alaska they followed a land bridge
to freezing cold Siberia,
sometimes moving, sometimes staying –
but the moving was in them.

Turning westwards from Siberia
their stumpy wings drove them on
all through Europe before reaching
the western fringe of Scotland.

Are your stumpy wings and your cocked tail
fit for a journey, little wren?
Or are your timid ways
keeping you back?

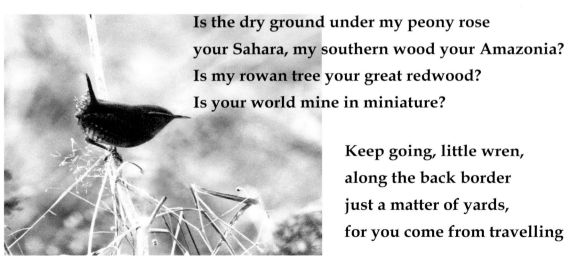

Is the dry ground under my peony rose
your Sahara, my southern wood your Amazonia?
Is my rowan tree your great redwood?
Is your world mine in miniature?

Keep going, little wren,
along the back border
just a matter of yards,
for you come from travelling stock.

Young Starlings

You don't know
as you squat, beaks wide open,
desperate to be filled,
you don't know you are destined
to catch your own
worms, snails and insects.

You don't know
as you squawk and chatter,
warble, rattle and trill,
you don't know you are destined
to higher things,
to gossiping on rooftops.

You don't know
as you pull out downy feathers
to make way for itchy new ones,
you don't know you are destined
to be lacklustre on dull days,
iridescent in the sun.

You don't know
as you flap,
testing your fledgling wings,
you don't know you are destined
to cloud together
swirling and swooping, twisting and turning,
dipping and diving in the ballet,
the great murmuration,
that can never be repeated
or forgotten.

Lullaby of the Eider

In the black silence
of the lonely hours
I hear another sound
woven together with the lapping
of the waves,
a soft sound
a cooing
– the lullaby of the eiders!

Their coos, melting into the waves,
rock me gently to sleep.

And so it is
that lulled by eider duck,
warmed by eider down,
I sleep till sunrise.